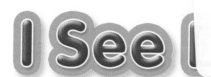

I See

Lisa Trumbauer
Illustrated by David Sheldon

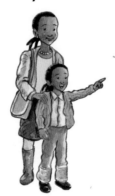

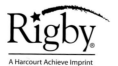

Rigby

A Harcourt Achieve Imprint

www.Rigby.com
1-800-531-5015

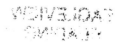

I see cars.

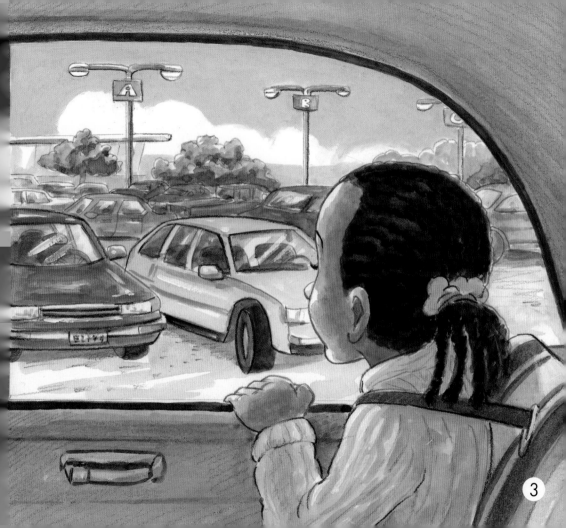

I see airplanes.

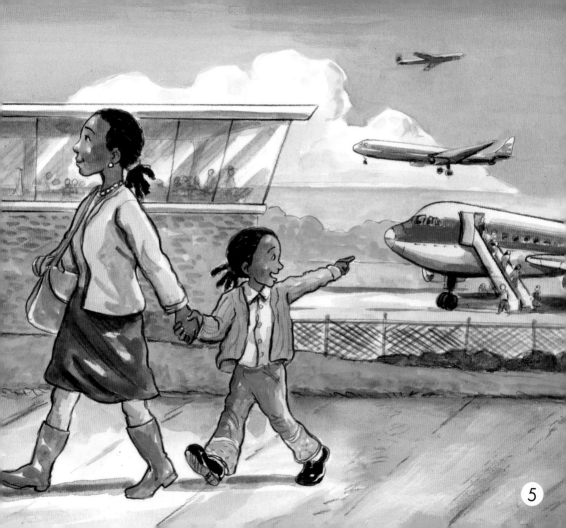

I see people.

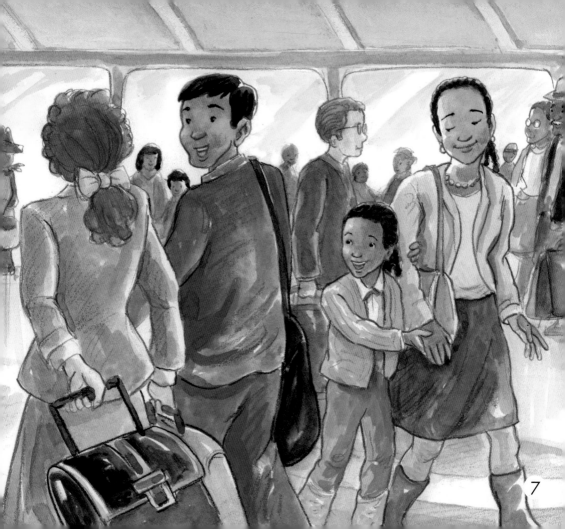

7

I see bags.

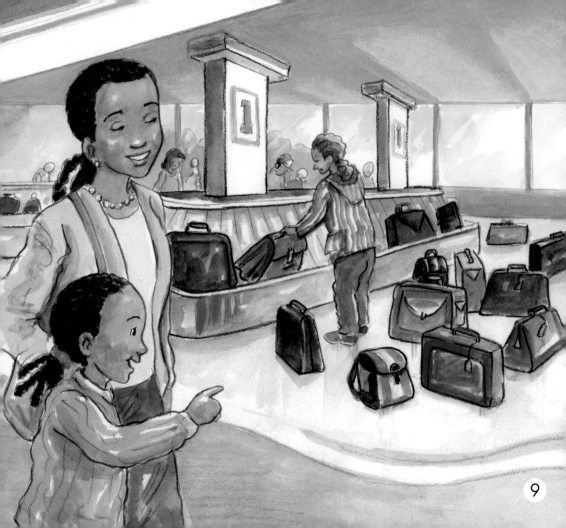

I see balloons.

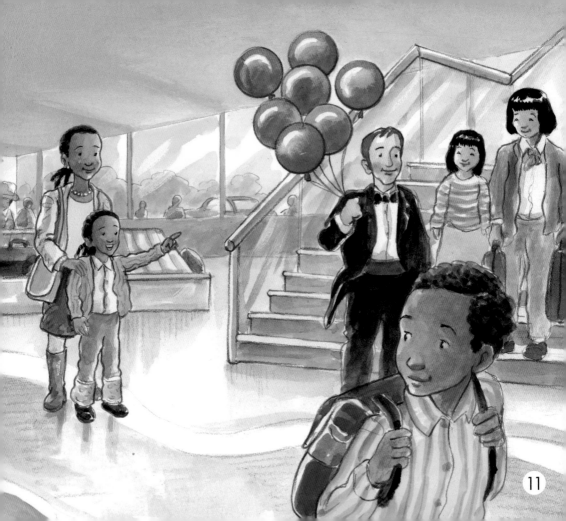

I see flowers.

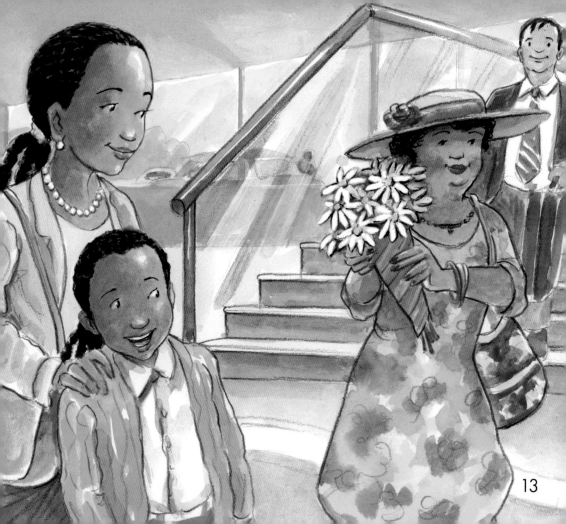

I see presents.

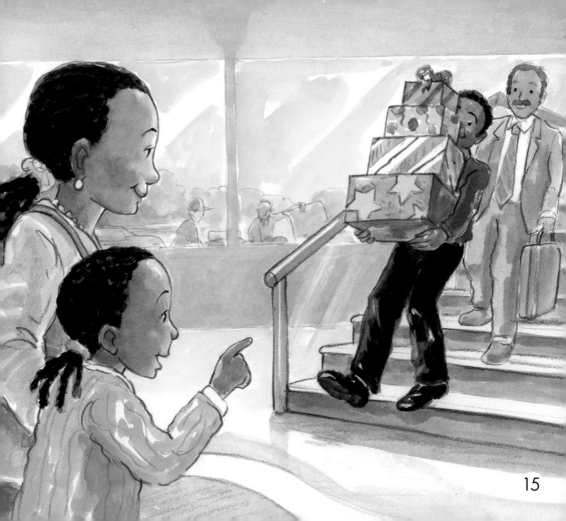

I see Dad!

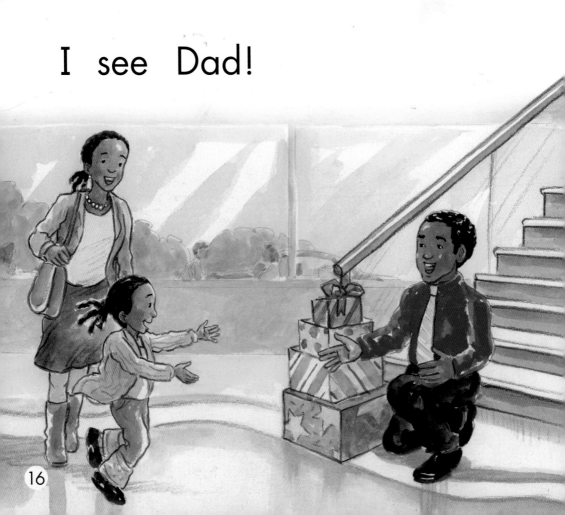